Support Systems

How Bones and Muscles Work Together

DEVELOPED IN COOPERATION

WITH

FORT WORTH MUSEUM OF SCIENCE AND HISTORY

FORT WORTH, TEXAS

Copyright © 1995 by Scholastic Inc.   All rights reserved. Published by Scholastic Inc.   Printed in the U.S.A.
ISBN 0-590-27618-2
1 2 3 4 5 6 7 8 9 10   09   01 00 99 98 97 96 95 94

THE HUMAN BODY IS MADE UP OF COMPLEX SYSTEMS
THAT INTERACT TO KEEP AN INDIVIDUAL ALIVE.

Support Systems

The human body has structures that support and move the body.

Read-Aloud

Support

Literature

B ones, cartilage, and ligaments form a skeletal system
that supports and protects the body.

Muscles connected to bones by tendons move the bones.

A person makes decisions that affect the health of
the body's support systems.

What Did We Learn?

What Supports Your Body?

What do you think you'd look like if all the bones in your body disappeared?

Look at these pictures of bones. Which bones belong to a human? a fish? a snake? a bat? How can you tell?

All the bones in an animal's body make up its <u>skeleton</u>. You can't see your bones, but you can feel some of them. How does your skeleton shape your body?

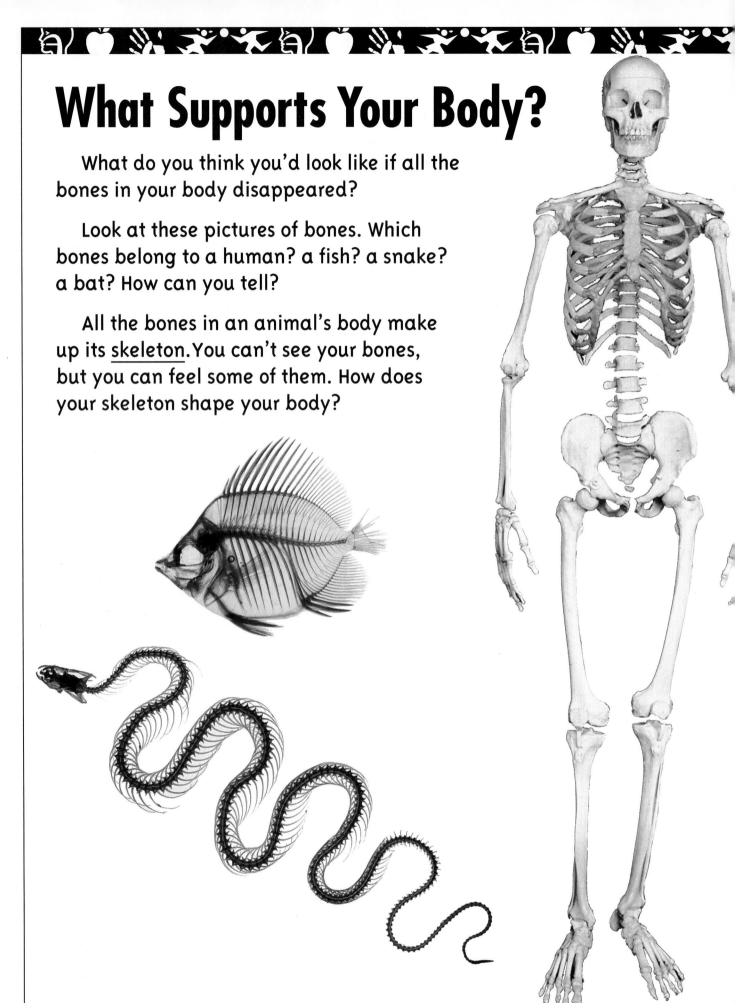

Get in touch with your bones.

❶ How many of your bones can you feel? Are they soft or hard? Which bones are long? straight? curved? Record your findings.

❷ Look at the model skeleton and try to find the bones you felt. What other bones do you see?

❸ Pick a bone you find interesting. What would you like to find out about it?

Bats are covered with skin and fur. Snakes and most fish have scales. People have skin. But they all have skeletons. How are their skeletons alike? How are they different?

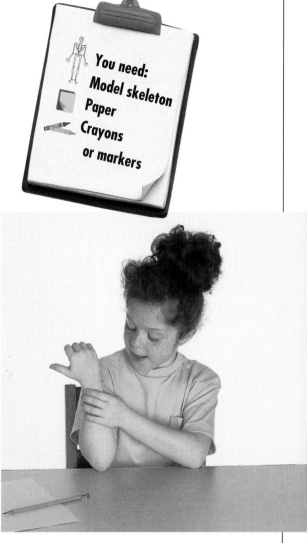

You need:
Model skeleton
Paper
Crayons
or markers

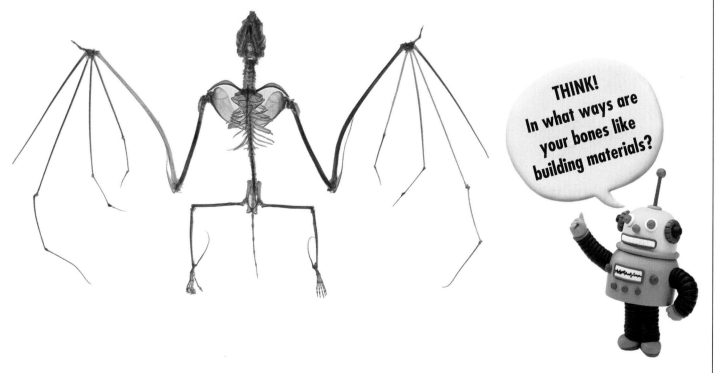

THINK!
In what ways are your bones like building materials?

5

What Are Bones Like?

Have you ever looked at the leftover bones from a Thanksgiving turkey or counted dinosaur bones at a museum? Maybe you've seen an Xray of your bones at the doctor's office.

What are bones made of? How are your bones like the bones of other animals?

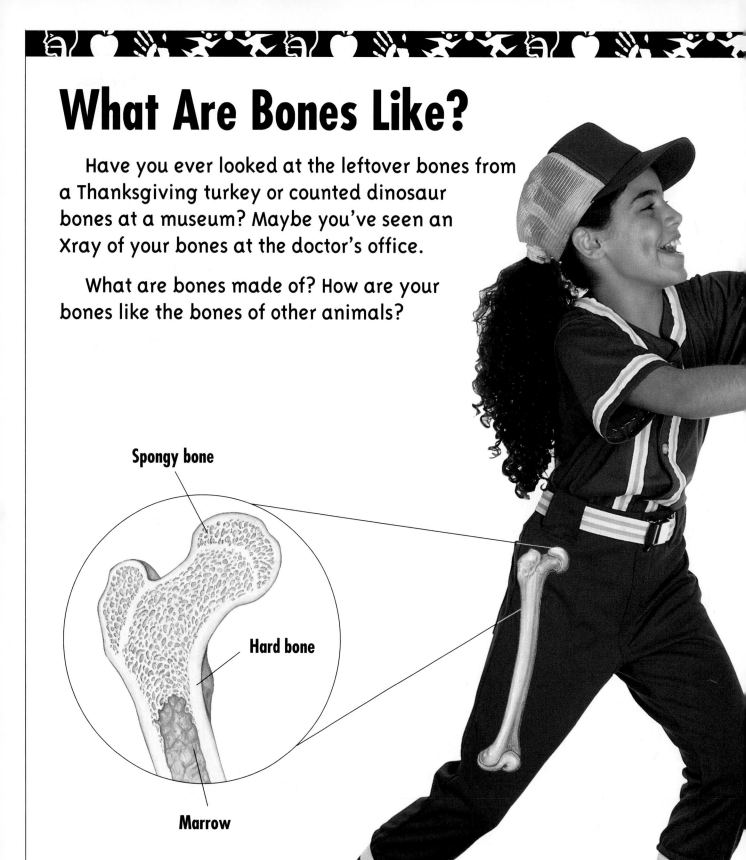

Spongy bone

Hard bone

Marrow

Meet a bone.

1 Examine a bone. Is it hard or soft? heavy or light? What is its shape? ✏️

2 Use your hand lens to look at the insides of the beef and chicken bones. How are they different? Describe what you see. ✏️

3 Compare the animal bones to the picture of the human bone. How are they different? ✏️

Bird bones are more hollow than human bones. Why do you think that's good for the birds?

You saw <u>marrow</u> in the bones you looked at. All the spaces in your bones are filled with a soft substance called marrow. Red marrow makes an important part of your blood. Yellow marrow is mostly fat.

You need:
Beef bone
Chicken bone
Plastic bag
Hand lens

THINK!
How would it affect your body if all your bones were solid all the way through?

How Do Bones Change?

Touch and wiggle the tip of your nose. Gently bend one of your ears. The bendable parts inside are made of <u>cartilage</u>. How does the cartilage feel? Before you were born, your skeleton was made up mostly of cartilage.

Look at the Xrays of the human hands. The dark color is soft cartilage. The light color is hard bone. How is the hand of an 18-year-old different from the younger hands? How do you think the bones in your hand will change as you get older?

3-6 months old

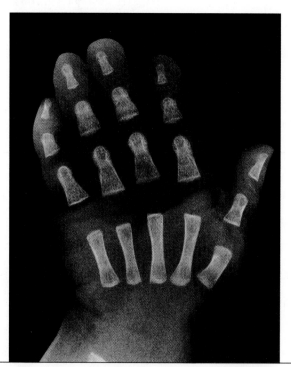

9-10 years old

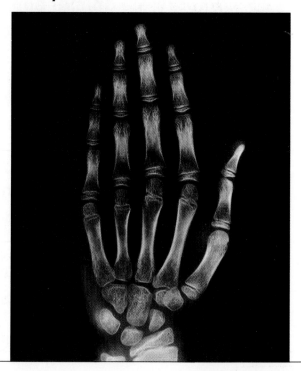

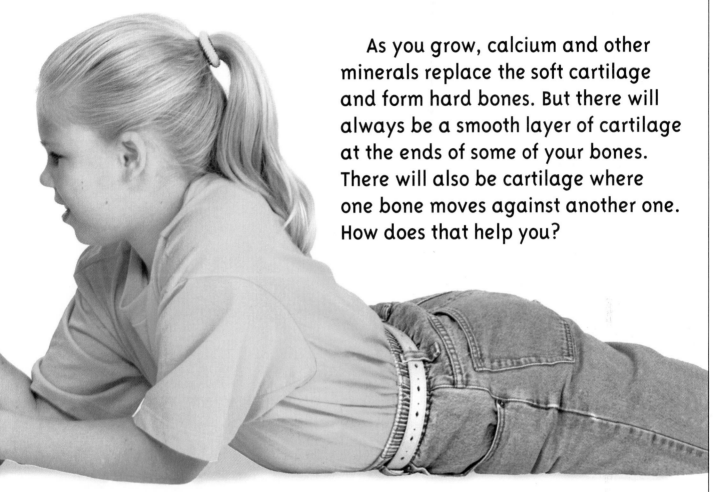

As you grow, calcium and other minerals replace the soft cartilage and form hard bones. But there will always be a smooth layer of cartilage at the ends of some of your bones. There will also be cartilage where one bone moves against another one. How does that help you?

18-20 years old

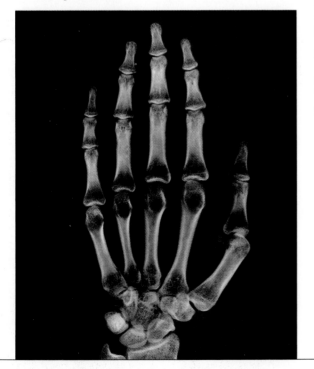

Your bones change every day. As you grow, many of them will join together. Most people have more than 300 bones when they're babies. But by the time they become adults, they'll have only about 206 bones.

THINK!
How could Xrays be used to figure out a person's age?

9

How Does Your Skull Work?

Bones change all through your life. But what they do stays the same. Think about your <u>skull</u>. What does it do for you?

You need:
Clay
2 plastic bags
Egg carton section
Tape

Pack it up.

1 Make two clay balls. Put one ball in a plastic bag.

2 Put the other ball in an egg carton section. Tape it closed and put it in another plastic bag.

3 Carry the two bags with you everywhere you go. Treat them like anything else you carry around. What do you think will happen to each clay ball?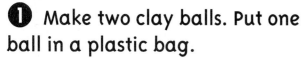

4 At the end of the school day, compare the two balls. What do you observe?

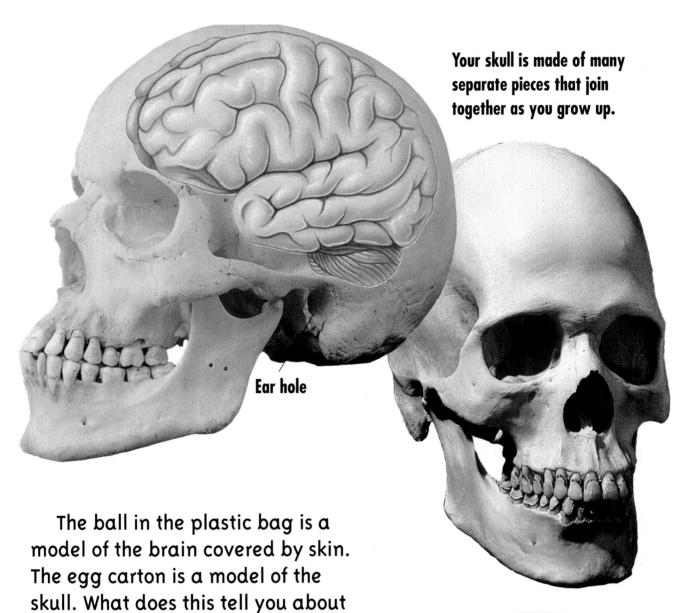

Your skull is made of many separate pieces that join together as you grow up.

Ear hole

The ball in the plastic bag is a model of the brain covered by skin. The egg carton is a model of the skull. What does this tell you about what the skull does?

Your brain is soft and delicate. It controls all five of your senses— seeing, hearing, touching, smelling, and tasting. It also controls all your body's activities.

Why do you think people sometimes wear helmets and hardhats?

THINK!
What is the only part of your skull that you can move? When does it need to move?

How Do Your Spine and Ribs Work?

Your skull has a special job. What do your ribs do? Think about the body parts in your chest. What part pumps blood through your body? What parts help you breathe? Try to feel these body parts. Why can't you feel them?

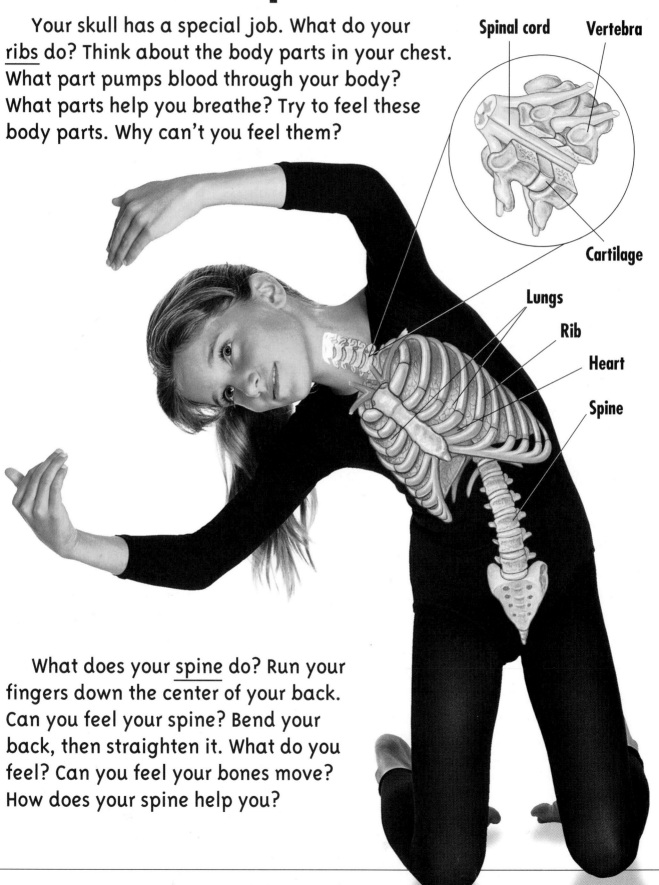

Spinal cord Vertebra

Cartilage

Lungs

Rib

Heart

Spine

What does your spine do? Run your fingers down the center of your back. Can you feel your spine? Bend your back, then straighten it. What do you feel? Can you feel your bones move? How does your spine help you?

You need:
Plastic straw

String
Scissors

String it out.

❶ Cut a straw in half. Put a string through one half. What happens when you try to bend the straw?

❷ Find a way to make the second straw bend more than the first. (Clue: Use the scissors.)

❸ Now put the string through the second straw. How does it bend?

The straw is a model of your spine. Your spine is made up of special bones called vertebrae. They're padded with cartilage. How do these bones help you move? How do you think the padding helps?

The string is a model of your spinal cord. Information from your brain travels through your spinal cord to all parts of your body. Why is your spine so important?

THINK!
Why is it better to have ribs in your chest instead of a solid shield like the skull?

How Do Your Long Bones Work?

You saw that different bones do different jobs. Look at the model skeleton. Where are the longest bones in your body? What do they help you do?

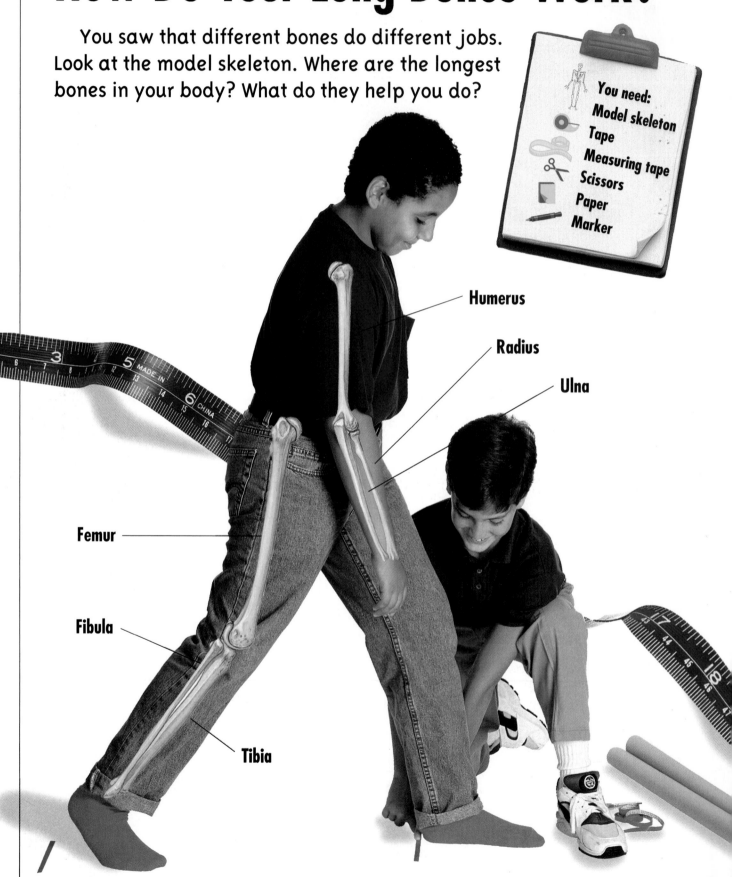

You need:
Model skeleton
Tape
Measuring tape
Scissors
Paper
Marker

Humerus

Radius

Ulna

Femur

Fibula

Tibia

Take a step.

❶ Mark where you stand. Then take as long a step as you can. Mark where you stop. Measure how far you went. What helped you step that far?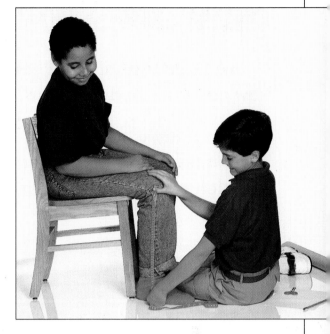

❷ Now measure the length of your upper leg and lower leg. These are the lengths of the long bones in your leg. Record and add the numbers.

❸ Cut pieces of paper as long as each bone. Label and tape them together. Cut a piece of paper the length of your step. Label it.

❹ Hang your paper strips side by side. Look at everybody's strips of paper. What patterns do you see?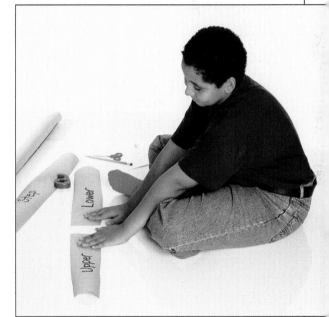

Your legs and feet and your arms and hands are called limbs. How do the long bones in your limbs help you?

The small bones in your hands and feet make up more than half the bones in your body. What do your small bones help you do?

THINK!
What bones in your lower limbs help you reach higher?

How Does Your Skeleton Bend?

Swing your arm. Bend your knee. Flex your finger. How can your body bend in so many different ways?

Your body usually bends where two bones meet. The places where they meet are called <u>joints</u>. The pictures show four kinds of joints and how they work.

Bend your body.

1 Locate places on your body that can bend. Move each body part. How does it bend and turn? Use the pictures to figure out what type of joint lets each part bend.

2 Make a table. List the places where you have joints and the kind of joint in each place. How many of each kind did you find?

Neck

Knee

Ligament

How Your Joints Move

A ball-and-socket joint moves the way a computer joystick moves.

A pivot joint turns like the hands of a clock.

A gliding joint slides the way the pieces of this puzzle slide.

A hinge joint bends the way a door hinge bends.

Bones are held together at the joints by <u>ligaments</u>. Ligaments are like strong rubber bands that keep a firm hold on the bones. Find them in the pictures of the hip and knee joints. Why do ligaments have to be strong and flexible?

Cartilage

Vertebrae

Ligament

Hip

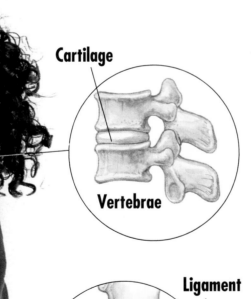

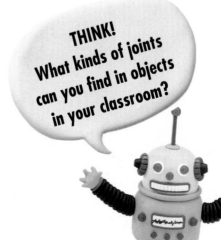

THINK!
What kinds of joints can you find in objects in your classroom?

17

What Makes Your Skeleton Move?

Your elbow joint helps your arm bend in the middle. But what makes the parts of your arm move? Place your right hand lightly on your left upper arm. Then make a fist with your left hand and move it toward your left shoulder. What do you feel?

You need:
String
Marker
Scissors

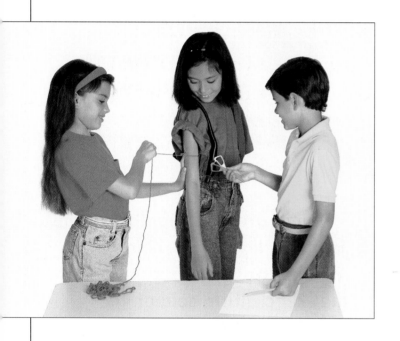

Make a move.

❶ Wrap string once around your partner's relaxed upper arm. Mark the string and cut it.

❷ Now have your partner make a big muscle and hold it. Wrap a new string around it. Mark and cut the string. Which string is longer? What happens to the muscles in your upper arm when you move it?

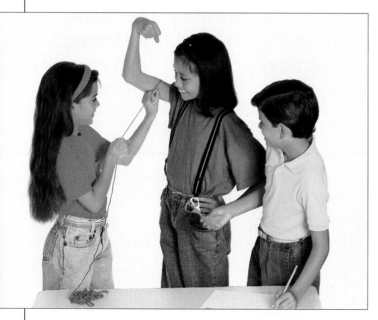

When a <u>muscle</u> is working to move your bones, it gets shorter, or contracts. When a muscle contracts, it bulges.

Your body has different kinds of muscles. The ones that help you move are the voluntary muscles. You can control them. How? They're connected to your bones by tough fibers called <u>tendons</u>.

Some muscles, like your heart, work on their own. They're the involuntary muscles. How would your life be different if your heart muscle didn't work on its own?

Tendon

Muscle

THINK!
What would your body be like if your tendons weren't doing their job?

How Do Your Muscles Work?

Your body has more than 600 skeletal muscles to move all your bones. How do they do their job?

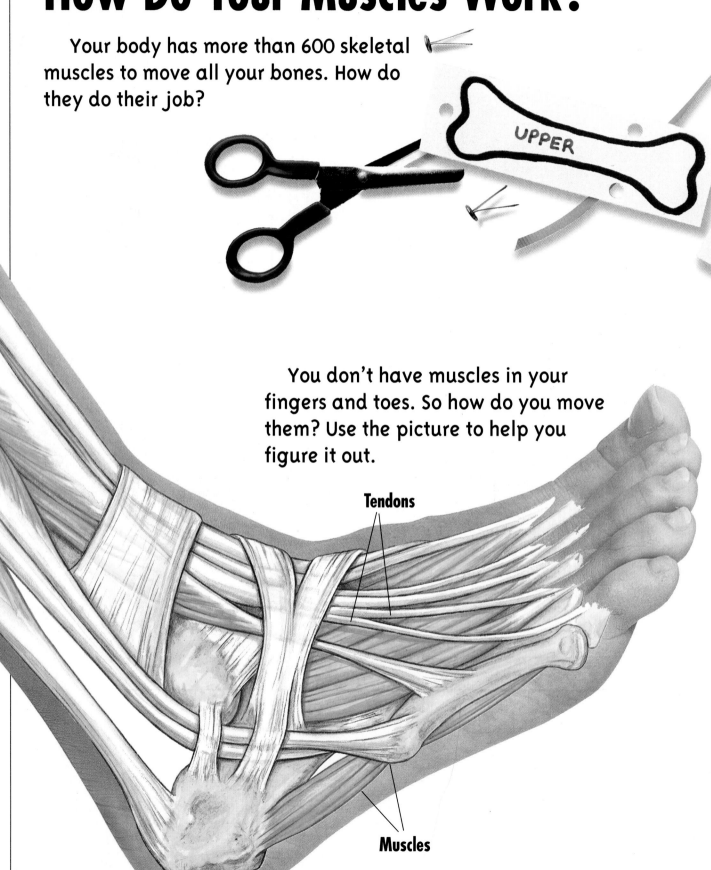

UPPER

You don't have muscles in your fingers and toes. So how do you move them? Use the picture to help you figure it out.

Tendons

Muscles

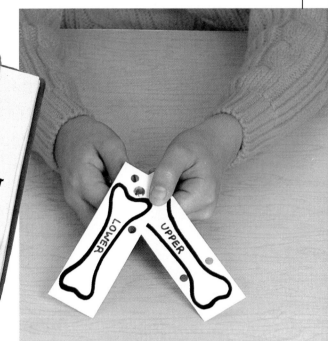

Make arm muscles work.

1 Cut an index card in half. Draw arm bones on the halves and label them. Punch three holes in each half, just as you see in the pictures.

2 Fasten the cards together. Tie a ribbon to each hole on the lower arm bone. Thread the ribbons through the holes on the upper arm bone.

3 Pull on the loose end of one ribbon. Then pull on the loose end of the other ribbon. Observe what happens to each ribbon. What happens to the bones each time?

Do muscles push or pull? Did both upper arm muscles work at the same time? How would your arm work if you had just one of the muscles?

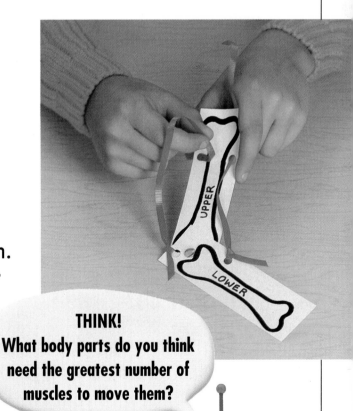

THINK!
What body parts do you think need the greatest number of muscles to move them?

What Are Muscles Made Of?

To help you move, muscles have to be strong. Even when you're sitting still, your muscles help hold up your head, chest, and back. What are these hardworking muscles made of?

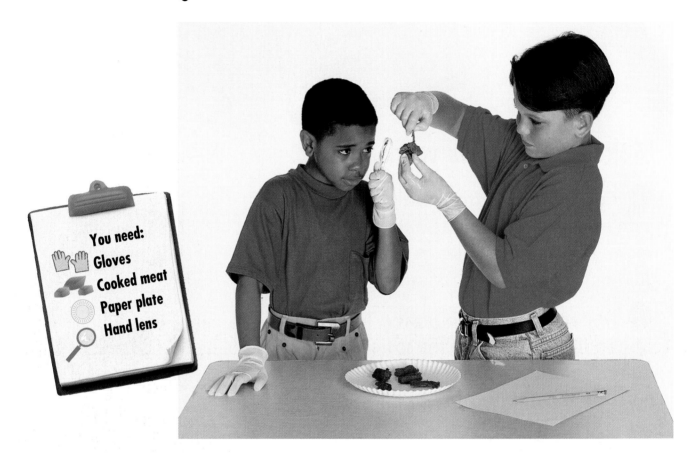

You need:
Gloves
Cooked meat
Paper plate
Hand lens

Tear it up.

❶ Put on your gloves before you handle the meat. Look closely at the meat. Then examine it with your hand lens. Compare it with the picture of muscle tissue. What do you see?

❷ Gently pull the meat apart. Describe what happens.

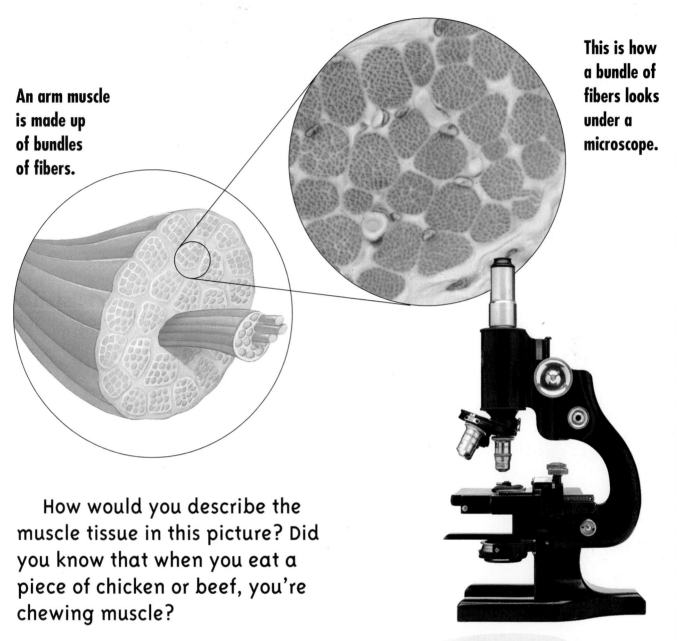

An arm muscle is made up of bundles of fibers.

This is how a bundle of fibers looks under a microscope.

How would you describe the muscle tissue in this picture? Did you know that when you eat a piece of chicken or beef, you're chewing muscle?

Most muscles are made of many long stringy fibers, blood vessels, and nerves. Blood brings the nutrients your muscles need to live and grow. Nerves carry messages that tell the muscles when and how to move.

THINK!
All your muscles together weigh more than all your bones. Why do you think this is so?

What Happens When Your Bones and Muscles Don't Work?

Imagine that your thumb bones and the muscles that move them no longer worked. How would that affect the way you did simple everyday tasks?

You need:
Chart
Tape

Work your thumbs.

❶ Try doing all the tasks listed in the table using your fingers and thumbs. Record your results.

❷ Tape one thumb to the palm of your hand. Now try doing all the tasks. Record your results.

❸ What did you find out? What happens when the bones in your thumb and the muscles that move your thumb no longer work?

People without full use of their limbs use other parts of their bodies to create things—like this painting.

THINK!
How are other parts of your body affected when you can't use your thumb?

Sometimes bones and muscles don't develop correctly. Sometimes they can be injured. If an injury is permanent, artificial limbs may help. But often, people must find other ways to meet the challenges caused by the loss of a body part. How did you solve the challenge of not having full use of your thumb?

How Does Exercise Affect Your Bones and Muscles?

If you've ever broken a leg or an arm, you know that the doctor puts it in a cast. When the cast is removed weeks later, it usually is difficult to move that limb. What happens to muscles while bones are healing? What do muscles need to stay in shape?

You need:
Chair
Clock or watch

Pump it up.

1 Sit on a chair and raise one leg. How long can you keep it raised?

2 Rest for a minute, then repeat step 1.

3 Rest again, and try step 1 once more.

4 Do this activity every day, and keep a table of your results. What differences do you see and feel at the end of one week?

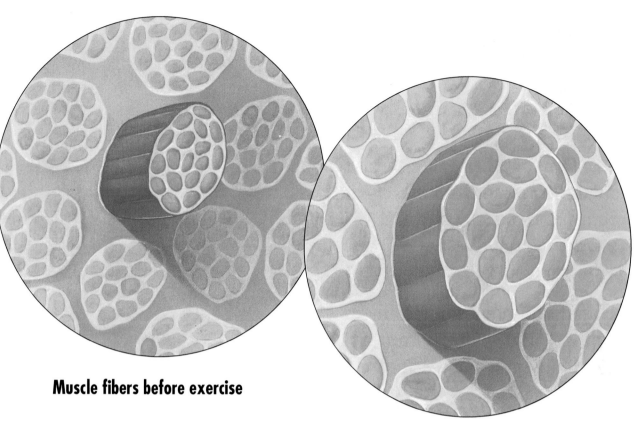

Muscle fibers before exercise

Muscle fibers after weeks of exercise

Muscles grow and change when you use them a lot. What change do you see in the muscle fibers in these pictures? What do you think happens to the fiber bundles and to the muscles themselves? What do you think would happen to your muscles if you didn't use them enough?

Exercise helps to keep bones and muscles strong. But rest and sleep are just as important to your body as exercise. While you sleep your bones grow and your muscles, tendons, and ligaments relax.

THINK!
How does posture, or the way you hold your body, affect your bones, muscles, and organs?

What Foods Are Best for Your Bones and Muscles?

You need more than exercise and rest for healthy bones and muscles. Your bones and muscles are made of proteins. So you need to eat a lot of proteins when you're growing.

You need Vitamin C for healthy muscles and bones. You also need vitamins D and A and minerals like calcium, fluoride, magnesium, manganese, and phosphorus for healthy bones. Calcium and phosphorus give bones their strength and light color.

How do you know if you are eating enough of the foods that are good for your muscles and bones?

You need:
Food labels

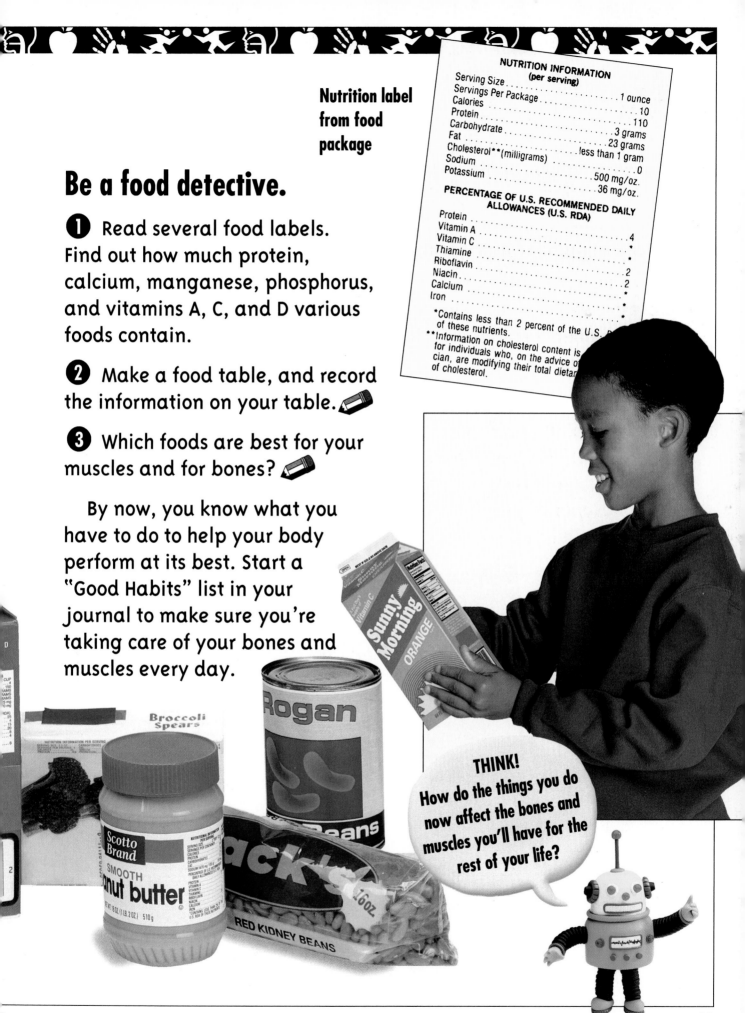

Nutrition label from food package

NUTRITION INFORMATION
(per serving)

Serving Size	1 ounce
Servings Per Package	10
Calories	110
Protein	3 grams
Carbohydrate	23 grams
Fat	less than 1 gram
Cholesterol**(milligrams)	0
Sodium	500 mg/oz.
Potassium	36 mg/oz.

PERCENTAGE OF U.S. RECOMMENDED DAILY ALLOWANCES (U.S. RDA)

Protein	*
Vitamin A	*
Vitamin C	4
Thiamine	*
Riboflavin	*
Niacin	2
Calcium	2
Iron	*

*Contains less than 2 percent of the U.S. [RDA] of these nutrients.
**Information on cholesterol content is [provided] for individuals who, on the advice of [a physi]cian, are modifying their total dietar[y intake] of cholesterol.

Be a food detective.

① Read several food labels. Find out how much protein, calcium, manganese, phosphorus, and vitamins A, C, and D various foods contain.

② Make a food table, and record the information on your table.

③ Which foods are best for your muscles and for bones?

By now, you know what you have to do to help your body perform at its best. Start a "Good Habits" list in your journal to make sure you're taking care of your bones and muscles every day.

THINK!
How do the things you do now affect the bones and muscles you'll have for the rest of your life?

How Can You Make a Machine that Moves Like a Body?

Healthy bones, joints, and muscles all work together. They make the human body move in amazing ways for both fun and work. But some tasks are too dangerous for people to do. Others require more strength than human bones and muscles have. What could some of those tasks be?

Engineers have invented robots to do work that people used to do or can't do. Most robots do the work of human arms and hands. Some robots are being used to explore other planets and the bottom of the ocean. What do you think robots are made of? What could a robot do for you?

Some robots perform dangerous work. How would a robot that lifts heavy objects be different from one that puts tiny electronic parts together?

Design a robot.

You need
Items such as:

Tubes

Straws

String

Rubber bands

Cardboard

Scissors

Hole Punch

Tape

1 Decide what you want your robot to do. Draw several stick figures to show how the robot will move.

2 How strong a frame does your robot need? What body parts will be like bones? What parts will be like muscles? What kinds of joints does it need?

3 Make a drawing to show what your finished robot will look like. Include a list of the materials and parts it will have.

4 Now try to build your robot. Does it work? Do you need to redesign it?

What do you think robots of the future will do? Maybe you'll help design them.

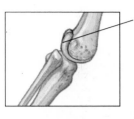

Cartilage: Cartilage is the firm, bendable tissue that covers the ends of some bones. Babies have a lot of cartilage; as they grow, bone replaces much of the cartilage.

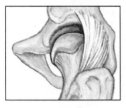

Joint: A joint is the place where bones meet. Hinge, ball-and-socket, pivot, and gliding joints are movable joints. They help the body bend in different ways.

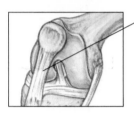

Ligament: Ligaments are the strong stretchy tissues that connect bones to other bones at their joints.

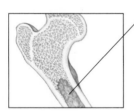

Marrow: Marrow is the soft material that fills the spaces inside your bones. Red marrow makes an important part of your blood.

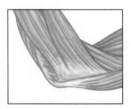

Muscle: Muscle is made of strong fibers that stretch and contract to move your body. The muscles you control are called voluntary muscles.

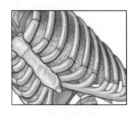

Rib: Ribs are the 24 bones that form a cage around the chest. Twelve ribs are attached to each side of the spine. The rib cage protects the heart and lungs.

Skeleton: A skeleton is the whole set of bones in a body. The skeleton supports all the other organs of the body.